WATER

PROTECT FRESHWATER TO SAVE LIFE ON EARTH

Written by **CATHERINE BARR**

Illustrated by **CHRISTIANE ENGEL**

Otter-Barry BOOKS

💧 For my friend Sophie, Frank Water Ambassador, who introduced me to the work of this inspiring charity in India and beyond – CB

💧 For Josie Rainbow – CE

Frank Water is a small organisation with a big mission: to restore and re-balance the global water system so that everyone, everywhere has access to enough safe water. Find out more at www.frankwater.com

With thanks to our advisor Peter Newborne, independent consultant and researcher – Senior Research Associate to the Climate and Sustainability Programme of ODI, a leading global affairs think tank. Peter carries out applied research on water policy and practice.

And thanks to Mike Morris, Former CEO, Severn River Trust, for useful and interesting expertise on fish ladders.

A catalogue record for this book is available from the British Library

ISBN 978-1-91307-446-3

Illustrated with mixed media
Printed in China

9 8 7 6 5 4 3 2

Contents

The first water on Earth

Earth began in a ball of fire. Our burning planet spun around its yellow star, the sun, and in time it cooled. Clouds formed and rain began to fall. Icy space rocks smashed and melted into this changing Earth.

SUN

CLOUDS

RAIN

SEA

This water has made life possible on planet Earth.

RIVERS

This first water collected in dips and hollows and stayed in sunlit pools. It flowed into wide blue rivers and trickled down into dark underground lakes. Most of the rain washed over salty rocks to become the deep blue sea.

The oceans filled up and this is how Earth became our blue planet.

COMETS

Face the facts

- Earth is the only planet known to have liquid surface water.
- These icy space rocks crashing into early Earth are called comets.
- Today 70% of the Earth's surface is covered in water.

Freshwater is rare

Most water is salty seawater. Just a tiny bit of all the water on our blue planet is freshwater. Today most of it is set in ice.

This water on Earth has frozen because, over time, Earth's climate has changed. Sometimes it has been very cold and during these ice ages the planet has been covered in ice and snow.

In the last ice age, snow packed down into the thick ice that still lies heavily on some land today. Glaciers fill high mountain valleys, and deep ice sheets sprawl across Antarctica and the Arctic island of Greenland.

These baby penguins were born on the ice sheet covering Antarctica.

Face the facts

💧 Only 3% of all the water on Earth is freshwater.

💧 Most freshwater on Earth exists in polar ice sheets.

💧 The Antarctic ice sheet is the biggest block of ice in the world.

💧 Today the world is getting warmer and ice sheets are melting.

The water cycle

All water comes from nature and moves in an endless journey between land and air.

The water cycle begins with the sun, which warms seawater until tiny droplets float up into the air. This water vapour also rises from plants as they breathe. High in the sky, these water droplets cool into clouds that blow over the land. Rising over hills and mountains, the droplets grow until they become so heavy that they fall.

The water cycle never stops. This means you might drink the same water that dinosaurs gulped 65 million years ago!

SUN

WATER VAPOUR

OCEAN

CLOUDS

RAINFALL

Dinosaurs splashed through ancient wetlands around the world.

WATER VAPOUR

melting ICE

RIVER

Face the facts

- Water has been recycling on Earth for over four billion years.

- A droplet of water can spend nine days in the sky and then from a few months to many hundreds of years moving through the water cycle.

- As water moves through the water cycle it changes between a liquid, gas (water vapour) and solid ice.

GROUND WATER

11

The colours of water

A glass of pure water is colourless but it is called *blue water*.
This is the life-giving liquid that tumbles down mountains,
crashes over waterfalls and runs over and under the land towards
the sea. Blue water is the liquid water that we drink and we can see.

Blue water seeps into soils and is sucked up into plants.
This hidden water is called *green water*. It flows up trees
into flowers, branches and leaves. All plants need green water
to survive and grow.

Animals, including you, are made of water too. This precious liquid is in our cells, our skin and even our bones. Water helps our bodies work and keeps us healthy and strong.

Face the facts

- You are 65% water!
- Most plants are 75% water.
- Natural freshwater is full of all kinds of invisible microscopic life.

These families are playing in one of New Zealand's many lakes.

Water is life

Freshwaters are home to a kaleidoscope of life. From muddy puddles, still ponds, lakes, wetlands and fast-flowing rivers, plants and animals thrive in very different watery homes. Frogs hop across waterfalls, hippopotamuses sleep in warm pools, fish dart down wide rivers and snakes weave through flooded forests.

All freshwater dwellers are part of food webs that spread beyond the water's edge. Across wide river basins other creatures too depend on freshwater to survive. Migrating herds of animals and flocks of birds cross dry continents in search of freshwater, and around the world huge wetlands teem with life.

But many of these freshwater habitats are drying up and disappearing. These wild, wet places are some of the most endangered habitats on Earth.

These dolphins diving into the Amazon river are an endangered species.

Face the facts

- Every form of life on Earth needs water to survive.

- Freshwater habitats are home to over 15,000 types of fish and over 4,000 types of frogs!

- Some animals, like salmon and eels, migrate between freshwater and salt water at different times in their lives.

The power of water

Water has incredible power. From the steady flow of wide rivers to crashing waterfalls and tumbling streams, it shapes our land. It smoothes rocks, carves valleys and creates landscapes where wildlife and people live.

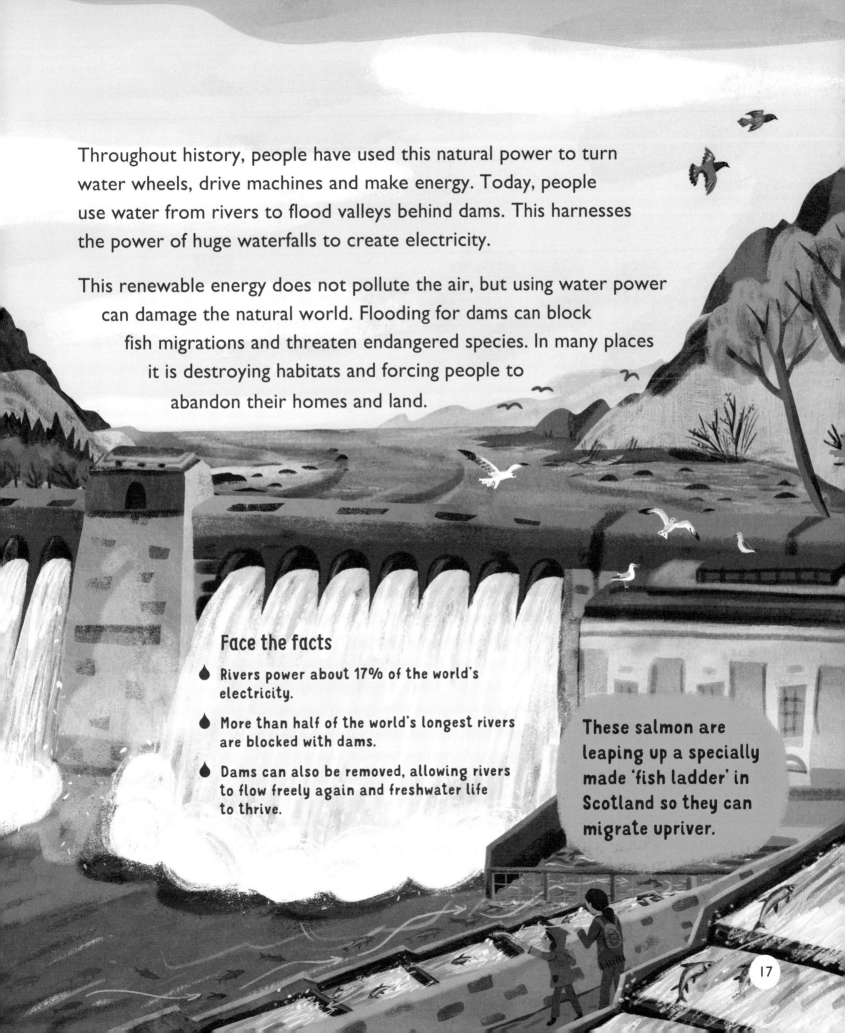

Throughout history, people have used this natural power to turn water wheels, drive machines and make energy. Today, people use water from rivers to flood valleys behind dams. This harnesses the power of huge waterfalls to create electricity.

This renewable energy does not pollute the air, but using water power can damage the natural world. Flooding for dams can block fish migrations and threaten endangered species. In many places it is destroying habitats and forcing people to abandon their homes and land.

Face the facts

- Rivers power about 17% of the world's electricity.

- More than half of the world's longest rivers are blocked with dams.

- Dams can also be removed, allowing rivers to flow freely again and freshwater life to thrive.

These salmon are leaping up a specially made 'fish ladder' in Scotland so they can migrate upriver.

Thirsty food

Farmers need water to bring seeds to life and to give animals to drink.
They watch the weather and understand the seasons.
Since farming began, rain and river water have been irrigating crops.

This family in California, North America, is watering crops which otherwise could not grow in this dry landscape.

18

Now, most freshwater on Earth is used in farming for food. But farmers everywhere are worried because weather is changing. Rivers are drying up, droughts are spreading and farmers are less and less able to rely on the rain. This is happening because of climate change.

Face the facts

- Climate change today is caused by human activities, adding gases to our atmosphere that trap heat on Earth.

- 'Greenhouse gases' are released when we burn fossil fuels, destroy forests, graze cows and grow their feed.

- Climate change makes weather less predictable and more extreme.

- Climate change threatens the survival of animals and people all over the world.

Enough water to share

If we use it carefully, there is enough freshwater on the planet to share. Yet around the world, poorer people have less than they need, mostly because big companies are taking too much.

Gigantic amounts of water are used to grow crops like cotton, sugar and palm oil. Freshwater is also taken from rivers to cool huge machines in factories, and to water golf courses and the gardens of luxury hotels.

These farmers in Mexico are harvesting sugar cane – a water-thirsty crop.

We need water to drink, wash, grow food, create energy
and use to make clothes and other things we need.
But like all other forms of life on Earth, we also need healthy rivers
and freshwater habitats to survive. Today, freshwater is unequally shared
and becoming more polluted, so it is often too dirty to use.

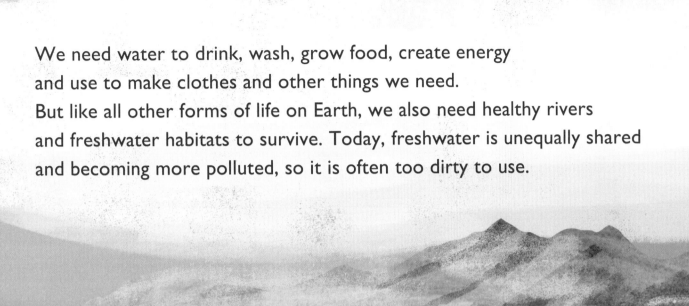

Face the facts

- 18 baths' worth of water can be used to grow cotton for one pair of jeans.

- There are 7.8 billion people on Earth and we all need clean water to survive.

- 844 million people lack access to clean water.

Pollution rising

Big factories and farms take freshwater from nature and pour out used wastewater. In many places heavy rainfall floods town and city drains. This means that they overflow with dirty water and sewage, which pollutes local rivers.

All over the world, rivers are also polluted by medicines being flushed away. Many contain chemicals that are harmful to freshwater wildlife.

These people in India are washing and worshipping by the Ganges, one of the most polluted rivers in the world.

Around the world, polluted water is spilling into freshwater habitats where animals and people live. It is poisoning the water people drink and killing freshwater wildlife.

Face the facts

- More than 80% of wastewater around the world is untreated, which means it may be harmful to wildlife and people.

- Every year millions of people are made ill by unsafe water.

- Scientists are investigating the threat to wildlife of rising levels of plastics in freshwater habitats.

23

Girl power

Many families in poorer countries do not have enough water. Every day, women and girls walk for hours to find and carry water back to their villages in heavy pots and buckets.

Often this water is polluted, so whole villages share dirty water that carries a real risk of disease. Droughts created by climate change cause even more water stress. Spending so much time collecting water means that girls miss school and millions grow up without a good education.

But simple wells and taps can bring clean water to rural villages, giving girls a proper chance to go to school and mothers the time to work. This makes families healthier and communities stronger. Access to water can change and save lives.

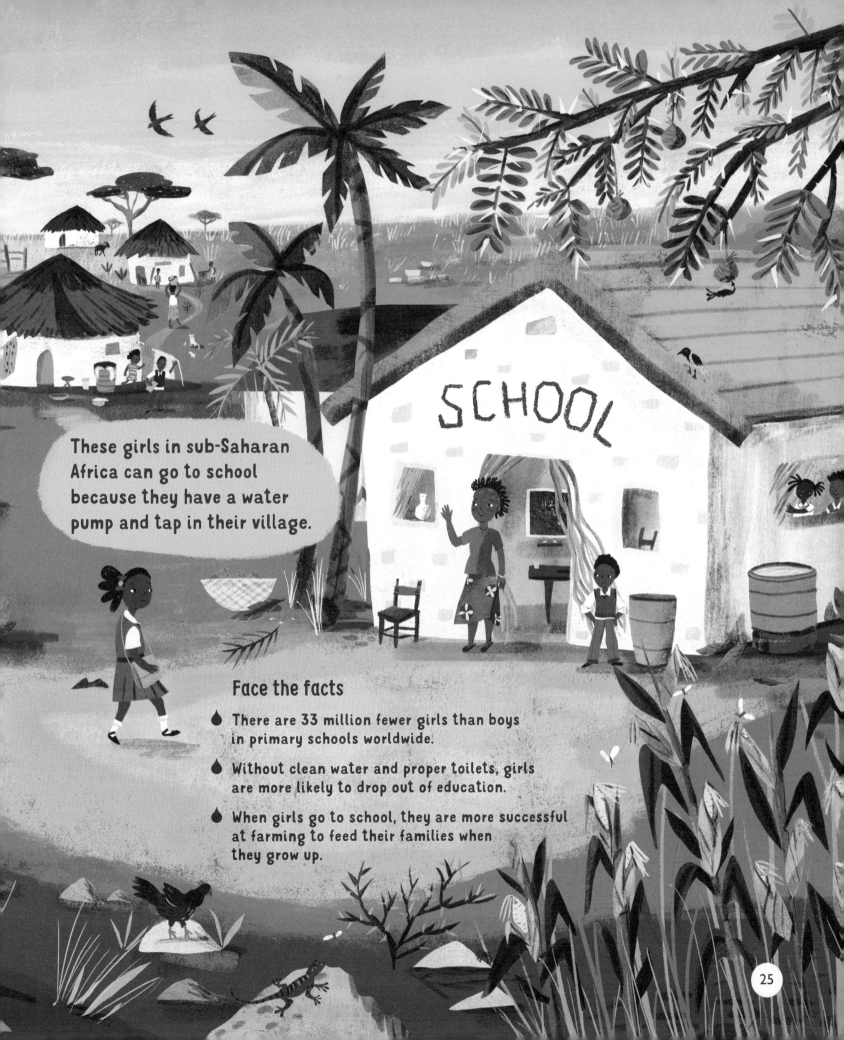

These girls in sub-Saharan Africa can go to school because they have a water pump and tap in their village.

SCHOOL

Face the facts

- There are 33 million fewer girls than boys in primary schools worldwide.

- Without clean water and proper toilets, girls are more likely to drop out of education.

- When girls go to school, they are more successful at farming to feed their families when they grow up.

Our precious water

Water is life. Freshwater springs, bubbles and flows with some of the most wonderful life on Earth. It makes up most of our bodies and, like all other forms of life, we completely rely on it to stay alive.

But today there is a freshwater crisis on planet Earth. As the human population grows, as our climate changes and rivers are polluted, it is more and more difficult for people and animals to find the clean freshwater they need to survive.

These protesters in Cape Town, South Africa, are asking farmers, businesses and families to save water to stop the city running dry.

Together, we can protect and share the precious freshwater on our blue planet. It's time to act – to make sure there is always enough clean water for all life on planet Earth.

Face the facts

- One third of all freshwater species are threatened by extinction.

- More than three quarters of all freshwater animals have disappeared since 1970.

- Only a tiny part of all the water we use is recycled.

- More than ten of the world's biggest cities risk running out of water.

A bath uses about 80 litres of water, but a shower only uses between 6 and 45 litres.

Using a fully stacked dishwasher saves more water than washing everything up by hand.

Most UK households flush the toilet 5,000 times per year.

Use environmentally friendly cleaning products.

28

Use a water butt to catch rainwater to water your plants, clean the car and wash windows.

Don't wait for the tap to run cold — save up to 10 litres of water a day!

- Eat less meat and dairy... A beef burger can take 15,000 litres of water to produce – that's 190 baths!

- Contact a local wildlife organisation to find out how you can help protect freshwater habitats.

How can I use water wisely?

- ## Take action to shrink your *water footprint!*

Recycle as much as possible!

Stop river pollution! Join a local river clean-up!

Explore your local freshwater habitats!

Make a small pond – you can use a big bowl for this – and create your own freshwater habitat!

- Almost everything takes water to make so so if we buy less, we shrink our water footprint.

- Visit your local river or lake to discover the animals and plants that live there... is it home to any endangered species?

- Use less plastic, recycle and re-use the things you buy, to reduce waste.

- Get involved – join a Climate Action Group!

⬥ It's Water Action Decade!

The United Nations (UN) has declared 2018-2028 Water Action Decade. That's 10 years' special focus to achieve safe and affordable drinking water for all by 2030.

LEARN Read this book to discover the story of freshwater around the world

SHARE Share this book with friends, family and school to start conversations about water

ACT Use the ideas in this book to save water and help protect freshwater habitats locally and globally

⬥ WORLD WATER DAY 22 MARCH
www.worldwaterday.org

⬥ WORLD TOILET DAY 19 NOVEMBER
www.worldtoiletday.info

Find out how you can help people save water in other countries too...
frankwater.com
wateraid.org

Find out more about how to protect freshwater...
www.wildlifetrusts.org/actions/how-conserve-water
www.friendsoftheearth.uk/sustainable-living/13-best-ways-save-water